HOPE FOR LOVE

A COLLECTION OF POETRY

ROB HILL, SR.

SPIRIT FILLED CREATIONS
BABU COMPANY

ISBN13: 978-1-7342948-1-1

Cover design by Donnie Ramsey

Published by Spirit Filled Creations/Babu Company
3509 Kids Court
Chesapeake, VA 23323

Printed in the United States

DEDICATION

I once dedicated a book to love…

I wrote:

"From this day forward,
I promise not to let the fears of my mind
force me to backspace the words from my heart."

I live by these words now, more than ever.

This book is for anyone
who has found love, lost it, and
discovered a better version of themselves.

I am learning as I grow
I don't know everything.
Well, anything…
I know everything changes, so
I'm ready for anything.
I will grow.

HOPE FOR LOVE

table of contents

INTRODUCTION

A few disappointments ago I lost all hope for love. I was ruled by emotion, maybe even hurting myself by living with a hopeless romantic mindset. I had no hope for a healthy relationship, a happily ever after, and certainly no hope for a safe haven with a partner in this lifetime. I decided that trusting myself was enough because depending on people left me stuck—not literally, because I always had the option of moving forward, just more so stuck willingly—wondering what was next for me.

Unsure of the future, I began to search within myself for some form of acceptance with the past. I was angry that some of my relationships ended with me feeling used and abandoned. It is never easy trying to bloom beside someone who feels stronger by ignoring your potential, purpose, and power. I learned to accept that some relationships were designed to teach me how important it is to grow with people who value me. Looking back on the past taught me to view life's journey as a marathon. The people who start with you may not have what it takes to finish with you.

Relationships change over time and through the years you will lose some of the people you loved the most. You won't lose them because you are a horrible person or because you're someone who's unbearable to be around. Relationships often change because loss is an inevitable facet of growth. Loss is a rough reality of life, but it doesn't have to be all bad because for every loss we experience, there is also a lesson attached. By learning to accept that the past can't be changed, I am now able to embrace both my light and my lesson. Embracing my light means that it is time for me stop holding myself back. It is time that I stop hiding my full personality, ignoring harmful habits, and downplaying my growth all out of fear of being deemed "too much to handle." I will never be too much for the person who was meant to grow with me. I don't know who I was expecting to grant me approval to love all of me, but I certainly wasn't gaining any confidence by looking for love from people who did not love themselves.

With time, I started the process of healing my heart. I became more aware that I needed discipline and accountability in my life. I started by forgiving myself so that I could release the past and all pain associated with it. Forgiving myself for what I did not know has been one of my biggest boosters in regaining my hope for love. I continued to heal by adapting healthier communication habits and improving my emotional reactions to disappointment, delays, and moments of distrust. Instead of choosing anger and resentment over minor issues, I learned to laugh and move on without giving away my power to anyone or anything. I've stopped looking for others to make my life better for me. You can't always control who you love, but you can control who you hold on to and with that, I accepted full responsibility to be the sole custodian of my joy and happiness. At times, seeking growth and healing left me feeling overwhelmed and exhausted at the thought of hoping for love another day. I got tired of things not going my way, tired of being overlooked for opportunities, and tired of failed attempts at pleasing people who were perpetually unsatisfied. I can't be something I am not just to keep someone in my life. I don't want a relationship if it has to be forced. I don't want to be hurt, and I don't want to be the reason for anyone else's pain. In order to release my fear and have peace of mind, I needed to take the most courageous step in healing my heart, which meant opening it up to learning new things again.

I believe we fall in love to learn life more intimately. I know that we find friendship with kindred spirits for divine purposes. We aren't just disposable time fillers in each other's lives. Our time together means something, even after growing apart. Knowing love, being loved, and even at times, losing love, keeps many of us searching for the meaning of it all. Our relationships teach us things we never knew we needed to learn and offer lessons that impact our lives forever. I want to leave people better than when I found them. I believe that is the purpose of my love—to inspire those who experience the most genuine parts of who I am. With each passing month, the more I gave, served, and listened, the more I began feeling more worthy of being loved. I knew I wanted a real relationship with trust, honesty, communication, safety, independence, partnership, fidelity, and mutual happiness. And I knew that I may not find that easily. I didn't want to avoid having basic expectations with people, but I did want to release all of my false expectations for relationships. Before finding my purpose, my only hope for love was that my process would be easy, but I'm fortunate to have learned that true love is worth phenomenal effort.

I am ready for love. I see many reasons to still have hope. I realize that life is full of teachable moments that either make or break us. So, when I get it wrong, I pick myself up, learn the necessary lessons, and keep moving forward. When I get it right, it confirms that I am in tune with my Creator, my purpose, and my assignment. I take leaps of faith daily, almost always uncertain of where my feet will land. But my heart is at ease knowing that what is meant for me will never miss me. When I reflect on how far I've come, I can honestly say that I'm doing well. I know that I am being prepared for something greater. As I continue to take life one day at a time, two things are always certain: I will never give up on loving myself and I will never stop giving authentic love to people. I hope this collection of poetry encourages you to have hope for love in your life again.

PART ONE

HOPEFUL IN MARCH

Ruled by emotion.
Unsure of the future.
Embracing my light.

HOPEFUL ROMANTICS

In times of uncertainty,
In moments of laughter,
In seasons of warmth,
In lifetimes hereafter,
Through breakups and breakdowns,
Promotions and resets,
Through trials and wrong turns,
Losses and regrets…
There we will be
You and me.
Both sound in mind,
together in spirit, and
rich in love.
Our legacy forever growing strong.

BE

Be the person you are trying to find.
Be the one with positivity and laughter, bringing patience and joy.
Be the one who is mindful to listen and willing to communicate.
Be someone who embraces change and is eager to grow.
Be supportive, honest, and self-aware.
Be the person you are trying to find.

LOVE

A commitment to protecting another person's heart
With same passion you use to guard your own.
A conversation about faith, forgiveness,
And finding strength to release a past we don't own.
A decision to always choose growth.
A reflection of understanding and hope.
Know love.
Give love.
Just love.

SAME OL'

It's nothing new with you,
And that's old to me.

AN EXCUSE TO BE MISERABLE

Don't make a thousand excuses for zero actions.
Failure defined in its simplest form is saying you can't do something
Before you have even tried.
Some people complain so much that all they have space to receive is more pain.
In order for you to have a breakthrough, you have to face what's in front of you.
Stop running
Do you want to be happy,
Or have you become comfortable with being unsatisfied?
Did disappointment teach you anything useful,
Or did it convince you that worrying and stagnancy was normal?
Have you forgotten that you could be active and growing?
Insanity is doing the same things over and over but expecting a different result.
You can choose not to change but don't be naïve enough to think things won't get worse.
Situations in your life won't improve until you start changing.
Stop looking for excuses to be miserable and start looking for reasons to value your life.
Growth may be challenging but now is not your time to give up.
You may be frustrated, depressed, and you may feel discouraged, but don't quit.
You have to be strong enough to see your process through.
Cry, scream, fight ...do whatever you have to do.
Find reasons to be thankful and eliminate all excuses to be miserable.
Finish strong.

WE'LL SEE

I can't forget the day you said,
"We'll see."
I finally understood why
we didn't need to speak.

BELONGS 2 U

It's been eight Tuesdays since we last kissed.
That's two months without seeing my favorite smile crack across your lips.
We made it through what most would dismiss as too much too soon.
But it was all us, the best of me and the real version of you.
Truth earned trust; my best view revealed through
That seventh Tuesday, when you told me
You loved me.
And that is a lot of time.
Everyday thinking of your love, your hugs.
Facetime can keep us close but ain't nothing like your touch.
You told me I should see what's out there
And yet all I can see when I look around is who is not here.
They are trying to fake everything you already naturally had.
But I adapt…I'm equipped.
See me, I'm focused on forever.
So, I can love you to infinity,
Or I can love you through eternity.
Just know there is nothing I won't do.
My heart
Belongs 2 U.

COULD HAVE

I could have loved you like that …
But I would have lost me.

WHAT'S IN THE DREAM?

What's in the dream?
See, I have found everything.
I have found my worst fears, colored with envy green.
This is me… this is me… see, I've found everything.

I found me…
I found love, flowing through everything.
I found me.
I found truth, maturing through everything.
I found me.
I found life, still choosing what's best for me.

What's in the dream?
See, I have found everything.
I have found my life's purpose, colored with golden rays.
This is us… this is us… see, I've found everything.

I found trust.

I found patience, growing through everything.
I found us.
I found forgiveness, recharging from everything.
I found you.
I found discipline, receiving what's meant for me.

What's a dream in action,
Like a plan in motion?
If you found everything, even pain,
Could your heart stay open?

TRUTH IS...

The truth is, none of us are easy to date, deal with, or please all of the time.
We all have our vices, attitudes, and way of doing things that make us who we are.
It's impossible to like everything about somebody.
Enjoying a relationship isn't about finding the perfect person.
It isn't about living some fairytale.
It's about finding something you're willing to work for
With somebody who is willing to work with you.
That simple.
Find someone who has a heart for you and never stop growing with them.

MAYBE

Maybe it's not supposed to be easy for you.
Maybe you're one of the few who can handle tough times
And still choose to be a loving person.
Maybe it's going how it's going because you're built for it.
Maybe you still have time to make a different choice.
And God would rather slow it all down and frustrate you
Than to let it keep going the way it is and fail you.
Maybe it's just your time to refine.
Maybe the pieces are being put into position and maybe it's not a test at all.
Maybe there is a future tailored specifically to what's best for you and rushing it could ruin it.
Maybe you're as different as you feel,
And maybe you'll stay strong long enough to teach people to feel the same about themselves.
Maybe we'll call it love.
Maybe this is just what your growth looks like in this season,
And it's okay to accept and love that person.
As long as you know you're giving it your all and the very best of you, keep going!
Don't stress a thing.
It's going to work out because you're not going to stop putting the work in.

WHAT'S YA LIFE LIKE?

Ever hear the story about the starving people who die smiling?

WHAT MAKES MY LOVE UNIQUE?

My love is persistent; it never stops wanting to give understanding, to better people, or to fulfill a purpose.
My love is detailed; it doesn't just exist, it loves past flaws, bad habits, and mistakes.
My love strengthens weaknesses.
My love is encouraging, it inspires, motivates, and broadens.
My love is not just good, it is necessary.
My love does not abandon, it endures.
My love is special because I am willing to do whatever I have to do to become that feeling you can't forget.
So, I give my heart to this world, not for attention or acknowledgement but because I am wealthy–I am full of love–and it is my duty to share it.
I am not perfect, so the way I love will not be either.
I have my ways and I could never promise a perfect relationship.
However, I know what's real and how to cherish something good.
And I know that when the right one comes along, that will be more than enough.

THANKFUL FOR THE RAIN

Nothing protects the heart like patience.
Don't get your hopes up too fast.
Don't let your fears speak too loudly.
Don't give your doubts too much time.
Not everybody is built to handle the tough times.
You can't be surprised when you outgrow flimsy relationships.
Few people understand what it means to really be there for somebody.
The hardest part of the journey is realizing that the main ones who said they would be there Until the end are often the first to fall off.
People make promises when the sun is shining and make excuses when the storm comes.
That is why I am always thankful for the rain—it washes away the unnecessary.

WHEN I GIVE

When I give, it does not come with strings.
I am not keeping track of what you owe me.
When I give, I choose to do so without ulterior motives.
I give because I know
What it's like to be without,
To long for and be ignored,
To speak and not be heard,
To care for and have nothing returned.
When I give it's because I understand.
It's because I know the value in what I have in my heart and
I refuse to let the world stop me from sharing that.
But when things start being taken for granted,
When you no longer appreciate my sincerity,
I won't switch up.
I will not get angry, and I will not be spiteful.
I will just get smart, and
I will change your role in my life.
Because when I give, I'm all in.
But when I am done, there is no looking back.

SOMEBODY'S DISAPPOINTMENT

We have all been somebody's disappointment at one point or another.
Still I am confident that I can contribute to someone's joy,
And I am committed to growing until it's time.
If you are quick to box me in, that's on you.
I don't feel it is necessary to prove to you that you are missing out.
I know who I am.
That is either going to be enough for you or it isn't.
When all is said and done,
You will see what is real.
You will see who is true.

LET ME TELL YOU ABOUT LOVE

Love does not lash out in anger.
If they do not care enough to guard their tongue,
They are not responsible enough to love you well.
Love does not shut down and close you out.
Love is not a deserter. Love is a fighter; it is a protector.
Do not confuse inflated emotions for love. Love is not just feeling—
Love is when feeling and action walking harmoniously.
It's easy to think dysfunction is love when you haven't been shown any better examples.
It wasn't love if it made you feel inadequate, rejected, and unappreciated.
You have to realize that people love based on their capacity.
Some people have a pint, others a liter, some a gallon.
You cannot expect a "pint person" to love at a gallon level.
With this understanding, you get how it is so easy for people
Who are full of pride, anger, and fear to walk away.
It is because they only have limited room for love.
And if you are somebody who has limited room for love, my life has limited room for you. No hard feelings, I have just been through enough to know my threshold.
I need that fulfilling, challenging, spontaneous, overflowing with passion kind of love,
And if this is not that, I know it is not for me.

NO PERFECT TIMING

Dating doesn't have to be hard; people are just so scared.
We say things like, "Love will find me,"
But that is just our excuse to stay closed off and not appear bitter or afraid.
The truth is, we need romance.
We all long for that connection and the opportunity
To be with somebody we don't have to hide from.
When the world is coming at you from all kinds of angles, it's nice to have a refuge.
Someone you can go to when you want life to feel "right" even if it's only for a moment.
There is no perfect timing You just have to be ready for that kind of comfort.

STEP OUTSIDE

At best, we are all just works in progress.
Perhaps you will never know enough to feel ready for all of life's surprises.
A relationship is about finding somebody you can grow with.
Somebody who knows you want to be whole.
Opening up won't kill you, it will heal you.
The more your fears control you, forcing you to shut down and hide,
The less authentic your love will be.
People can't find and connect with parts of you that you are not willing to show.
Don't ruin a potentially good thing being stuck on the bad memories from your past.
Step outside of you comfort zone, and
Always remember: A chance is a terrible thing to waste.

PRAYING FOR US

If you are doing well I pray things only get better for you.
If you are looking for answers, I pray clarity and understanding for you.
If you are questioning your relationships, I pray you have peace of mind.
I pray you are open enough to recognize and accept what is best for you.
If you are lost, I pray you have increased awareness.
I pray you are surrounded by people who remind you of how great you were born to be.
If you are hurting, I pray restoration comes to you.
I pray you are given the strength to let go, the courage to move forward,
And the time you need to heal.
If you feel like quitting,
I pray you are given a vision that shows you beyond today's circumstance,
One that inspires you to keep going.

PLAYING FOR KEEPS

Crazy how life works.
The best people get hit with the worst of times.
The genuine hearts are the first to be used and taken for granted.
And those with sincere intentions are pushed off as too good to be true.
We're stuck in a game where winning gets you nowhere worth going.
We have inconsistent people expecting consistency.
Liars complaining that nobody is truthful.
Fakes demanding loyalty.
Everybody is asking for love, but only a few are walking in it.
For me, the game got old two disappointments ago,
And I refuse to cheat my future worrying about things I can't change from my past.

So today in the present, I offer three promises:
I will trust you until you show me that I can't.
I will be as consistent as your efforts inspire me to be.
And I will honor your time with the same respect I give my own.
No games. No gimmicks. No guile.
If you can appreciate this, I can build with you.
If not, I have no time for you.
I have been through too much to play the same old game,
Just to keep getting the same results.
I want more, I deserve more.
So, I am holding out until I get it.
Because next time I play, I am playing for keeps.

LOVE YOURSELF

Love yourself enough to let the ones who are not willing to step up, miss out.
Love yourself enough not to sell yourself short with the bare minimum.
Love yourself enough not to give up on the days you feel discouraged.
But I understand…
Love is not for everybody in this season.
And I respect that.
All I ask is that you respect my time, my effort, and my heart.
Love yourself enough not to play games.
Simple enough, right?

EVEN IF IT HURTS

Just be smart enough to know when enough is enough.
You can't complain about somebody crossing the line when you failed to set boundaries.
Don't complain about somebody wasting your time when you didn't require them to earn it.
Sometimes, you just have to let go.
Not everything is meant to be a forever kind of thing.
You have to be honest with yourself, even if it hurts.
You don't owe them more chances to make the same mistakes.
Learn from the choices.
Grow out of old behavior.
Be done with repeating negative patterns.

THE BEGINNING

You know what makes the beginning so dope to us?
It is the excitement of knowing you have something worth looking forward to.
In the beginning their flaws don't provoke you to anger
Because you are focused on working with them and building the team.
But once the bond is tested and rough times come, we clam up.
No more building the team. Now it's all about placing the blame.
The speed of our generation has ruined our ability to treasure relationships with substance.
Very few of us know how to help improve others;
We only know how to replace what's not working with what we think is the next best thing.

We go for what's easy, not what is really worth our energy and effort.
But secretly we all long for that someone who gets us eager.
The one who has us checking our phone randomly hoping there is a message.
We all want that person who makes love hard to lose.
We are scared to admit that we don't know how to get to the happily ever after we imagine.
We are scared to have to find a new way.
It's a new game of chess in this generation when it comes to love.
Us kings and queens are on our own, and
I pray we protect each other.

FEELING ACKNOWLEDGED

There is something magical about feeling
acknowledged and valued.
To be welcomed with fresh eyes and open ears,
Just because they appreciate the way you sound
When you talk about the things you care about.
Feeling understood is uplifting.
We breathe easier when we know we are around somebody who has
"Been through it too."
Somebody who cares
To learn who you really are
Without making you feel wrong for the mistakes that come with just being you.
Making that connection matters.
It affirms the power of love.

THE HARDEST PART

The hardest part about wanting something real
Is trying to convince everybody you're not crazy for feeling like you deserve it.
But then you realize, you don't have to prove anything to anybody.
All you have to do is…
Be patient enough to make it right.
Be committed enough to make it strong.
Be honest enough to make it last.
Genuine people deserve something great. We deserve something authentic.
And we reserve the right not to be impressed with the usual.
It's not about being too picky or having unrealistic expectations.
It's about knowing you've dealt with enough people
Who do not measure up to what's best for you
And you've earned the right to have a preference.
Stay true to you even when nobody gets it.
Trust your heart even when you are scared.
Believe in love even after you've been hurt by people who did not believe in you.
Things get better the minute we stop expecting them to be perfect.
Timing is everything, so always remember that
Some amazing things can happen when you mix patience with hope.

PUTTING IN WORK

The whole process of putting in the work is tough.
What you get in the end isn't always what you thought you were working towards.
I see why so many people are hesitant to put effort forth in relationships

Because these days, it's rare to get anything back.
People say they want you to be true, but they aren't even honest with themselves.
At times I feel trapped in a world full of shallow people who lose interest fast

Because they lack the substance required to keep anybody's attention.
Nobody wants somebody who doesn't seem to value who they are
And what they have worked to become.

That's why when you come across somebody different, a person who values your journey,
It's so important to appreciate the chance since you never know when it's coming back.

Who doesn't want somebody worth investing in?

Somebody you can build with and not have to constantly worry about their loyalty changing?
Sad to say but it's almost as if all the good ones have given up on finding a good one.

Hope For Love

Many are scared of love, too ego consumed to work for a healthy relationship,
And so full of pride that growth potential doesn't matter anymore.

Maybe most have given up, but that's not me.
I know my partner is out there and I'm going to keep getting better until we meet.

I pray you have the strength to do the same.

LOVE YOU PERFECTLY

Nobody can love you perfectly. We're human and we make mistakes by nature.
But there is somebody who can love you unconditionally—pray for you, help you,
Support you, and genuinely care for you as consistently as you need them to.
The key is, you have to let them.
Stop holding back in the present just because you got hurt in the past.
There is more to life than pain,
But that's all you will ever know if you keep avoiding opportunities to grow.
When a relationship is real, it won't be perfect,
But if you are willing to work at it and open up, it could be everything you've ever wanted.

CAN'T TELL THEM

Can't tell them they're worth it and then quit on them.
Regardless of how hard it is.
"You're worth it," implies that you know there is work involved
And you're committed to sticking it out.
Don't let your ego cheat your heart.
If the connection is special, real effort will be required to keep it that way.
Pride has been the cause of more broken hearts than love.
That guard you have up may be blinding you more than it is protecting you.

SOMEBODY WHOSE LIFE INSPIRES ME

I just want somebody whose life inspires me.
I want a bond I don't need a break from.
And if it takes a while to build, so be it.
I'm patient because I know what's ahead is worth it.
I'm not one of those people who wants a relationship just to have somebody.
I want something strong, so I choose to move slow and I don't show too much.
But it's not to push people away. It's more so to see who is worth letting in.
I'm not here for a fairytale, I'm here for a forever.
And I'm cool if only a few understand that.

WHAT MY HEART DESERVES

Honesty, trust, respect, and loyalty.
We all have these basic expectations,
We just lose hope because we make exceptions for basic people.
We lack the discipline to wait for that extraordinary one.
In relationships we all share very common desires:
Be consistent,
Keep your word,
Don't lie…
We just differ in our approach.
Regardless of our fears, our flaws, and our past,
We all have more in common than we think.
Who doesn't want to be adored, valued, and loved?
Who, besides a hurt or scared person, wants to be alone by choice?
It's unnatural.

Hope For Love

When the love is good, there's nothing like it.
And you can tell who has never really been loved before, because no matter how it ended,
A person who has truly been loved still believes in it.
But maybe you will never know how beautiful your heart can be
Since you're too scared to let it go through anything.
All I know is that there is nothing like having something good with somebody you can trust, Grow with, and learn from.
I don't care how much the process hurts,
I'll persevere through it all because I know what my heart deserves.

SHE'D NEVER BEEN

She'd never been undressed before by words alone.
She couldn't fathom how a stranger could make her feel so at home…
He intrigued her
In the absence of touch, smell, or sight.
He became the most vivid part of her imagination.
He made her feel understood,
And in a way she never knew she longed for…
His voice arrested her, and she trusted his direction…
She knew he could handle being in control…
And she'd be waiting for that.

HEAVEN'S RECIPE

The weather called for rain.
I hate moving on those days.
If joy comes after pain,
I think I'm due for a parade.
Night brings the light here
Stars remind me of your eyes
Finding love is never fair
But you've showed me cloud nine.

Finally embracing my freedom
Your love takes me high,
Said I was dumb for leaving them
Your heart showed me why.

And now,
I don't want it all. I only want's good for me.
You stepped up when I called, me and you,
Heaven's recipe.

FIRST DATE

I talked to God about you again today, and
He said us finally meeting made Him smile.

PART TWO

DOUBTING BY JUNE

Becoming more aware.
Feeling overwhelmed.
Searching for meaning.

TEN STEPS

Just 10 steps.
That's all it took
For me to feel it.
Your smile, that look,
This moment was heated.
Full lunar eclipse,
A new phase was needed.

BUT

But,
Before I open up,
Can I tell you how to love me first?

TELL ALL

I'll never tell all.
Couldn't do our love like that.
Won't ever tell all.
Refuse to do our past like that.
But if I tell y'all,
Respect my trust like that.
See I was well off,
Before I chose love like that.
I said I'd never tell all
I'll never tell…
Until I told y'all.

MORE THAN THEY CAN HANDLE

When you are strong, you are too much of a challenge.
When you don't need them, they don't want you.
It's all manipulation…
Lord forbid a situation require you to be patient, grow a little more, and experience new things.
Is that just too much to ask for?
For most it is, "take me as I am," and be frustrated when I don't grow.
Nah, I will see you for what you are, but I am taking you for what you can become.
I need to make sure we can grow together.
If you are the type of lover to run when life gets hectic, I have to let you go.
This is why we all have to be careful about what we wish for.
What you think you want may be more than you can handle.

LOYALTY IS BUILT

Loyalty is built on trust.
If you are one of those "trust no one" type of people,
I can't let you get close because it's only a matter of time before you switch up on me.
I don't play games.
I don't do "sometimey."
I don't respect the love unless it's unconditional.
It's three things I need:
Trust, loyalty, and consistency.
If any of those is hard for you,
I'm not the one for you.

NOTICE

I may not speak on it all, but I notice everything.
These mental notes have always been on point.
I have never been naïve.
Don't underestimate what I know just because
I am selective about what I share.
People think that just because you don't try to catch them in every single lie
That means you aren't paying attention.
That's a mistake.
I don't play detective, set traps, or any of that.
Time reveals all!
Eventually everything comes to the light.
Your actions dictate our relationship.
I don't keep people in my life who haven't shown me they deserve to stay.
The little things add up.
Always remember that.

NEVER FORGET

You will never forget
The one who saw something in you that the rest didn't…
The one who didn't quit on you.

YOU CAN'T FORCE LOYALTY

You can't force loyalty.
Some people will always let you down.
Everybody won't always be who you want them to be.
People are consistent with who they want to be consistent with.
They are true to who they want to be true to.
They are loyal to who they need to be loyal to.
It's all about choices.
In my life,
Every excuse just gets you closer to an exit.
And it's no love lost.
I just choose not to waste my time with the games.
We can be cool, we just can't be close.

I'VE GIVEN UP

I've given up on trying to be anybody's dream,
I've had to endure too many nightmares myself.
I can be your…
Friend,
Confidant,
Motivator,
Support system,
Refuge,
Peace,
And more.
I just can't be your fairytale because
It would require me to be a lie.
All I can be is my…
Genuine,
Flawed,
well-intentioned,
Mistake-prone self.
May not sound dreamy,
But at least it's real.
"Me" is all I know how to be,
It's all I care to be,
And that's going to have to be enough.

KNOWING WHAT YOU DESERVE

Knowing what you deserve is pointless
If you aren't patient enough to wait on it
And disciplined enough to work for it.
Trying to force it equals settling.
There is a difference between putting in work and wasting time.
You should be getting something that makes you better out of your situation.
Be aware of what you are giving yourself to.
You can't expect a return if you're investing yourself in dead relationships.
The desire for things to be easy is the
Main reason people rarely get anything worth keeping.
Take a chance and try a new approach. Besides,
When the chemistry is gone, the history doesn't matter.
It may hurt to let go, but you have to
Do what's best for you.
Trust me, you will be okay!
It's amazing what time can do to even the strongest of feelings.

IF IT'S SPECIAL IT WON'T BE EASY

Life might not make sense right now.
It may seem pointless like nothing is changing, but you can't give up now.
You've given too much. You've grown too much.
You have sacrificed too much. Don't stop now.
You've come too far to quit.
It's not going to be easy and it won't always be fun, but you have to persevere.
Breakdowns lead to breakthroughs when you're diligent enough to keep going.
You have to be willing to fall and get up, to fail and try again, to be told "no" but keep working.

If it's special, it won't be easy.
Without a trial there is no triumph.
You don't deserve the great if you quit every time things don't go your way.
You can't be the champion if you run from the challenge.
There are two types of people in life:
Conquerors and complainers.
The conquerors find a way,
The complainers find an excuse.
When you want something bad enough and you know you deserve it,
You don't stop until it's yours.
Though quitting is at times a thought in my mind, it will never be an option in my life.
I will win…
I have to.

I JUST WANTED TO BE THE ONE

I just wanted to be the one
Who made everyone one of your disappointments feel like a blessing in disguise.
The one who fought for you when the rest were against you.
The one who made the effort when everybody else made excuses.
I wanted to be all that and more, but
You wanted me to perfect.
You wanted an excuse to run because you were scared you wouldn't be enough for someone like me.
You wanted something good, but your fears had you trying to control every little detail
And that is what stopped us from building something great.
After a while a good heart starts realizing it can't be in love with a quitter.
It no longer beats itself up about leaving too soon.
It learns to accept an ending.
A good heart learns the difference between moving forward and walking away.

YOU HAVE TO LOVE, LOVE

You have to love, love.
You have to love the opportunity to share the best and worst of you
With somebody who still wants to be with you no matter what.
You have to love the chance to be valued, appreciated, and adored.
You have to love the gift of being understood, balanced, and treasured unconditionally.
You can't hold on to every mistake or judge every flaw.
You can't expect perfection or cloud nine all the time.
It's unrealistic.
Love is perfect.
Unfortunately, the way we express it never will be, and that's why
Love is only for forgivers.
A bitter heart can't get better. It blocks its own healing.
Be realistic with yourself and fair to your heart.
Do your actions correlate with your expectations?
Are you really willing to open up and put the work in?
Or are you so pressed to have a fairytale
That your emotions and pride are blocking the possibility of you finding your forever?
For me, I remain hopeful in the midst of my patience.
I've earned the right to be excited about what's ahead.
I'd rather work to have happiness
Than settle with the ifs and regrets that come from being too scared to try.

THIS HEART

It wasn't about being selfish, or scared, or any of that…
It was the fact that pain was all too familiar to this heart.
And from this point on it was either
Commit to staying around or
Be incredibly great at staying away.
No in between, no room for lies, no tolerance for the back and forth.
After a while you get tired of getting your hopes up just to be let down,
So rather than force it,
This heart decided to wait…
And wait…
Until things were right.
Because when something real came around, this heart would be ready.
And that's all I'm focused on.

MANTRA

I trust my ability to know what's right for me
Without having to doubt who I am when I get things wrong.
I realize there is always room for improvement and
I commit to consistently trying to become a better person in all aspects of life.
I'm not better than anybody.
It's just clear that I am not the same as everybody.
And I work within my purpose every day to make that clearer.
Greatness is what I choose for my life,
Therefore, I make no excuses when I fall short.
I only put forth more effort.
I'm here for something bigger than me, and
My only desire is to add value to everything that I can.
Should I stumble, I will remember who I am, and
I will remember that my mission is more important than my mistakes.
I will never quit.

DEDICATED

When it's all said and done, I want to say that I made no excuses.
I did whatever I had to do to make it happen.
Everybody won't understand what you're doing,
Why you're doing it, and where you're trying to go.
And that's okay! Just focus on getting there.
You can't be afraid to separate yourself.
People recognize results. They don't get it unless they see it.
Be good at what you do and find ways to consistently get better.
The rest will handle itself.

FAITH TALK

Everything that is happening right now is happening for a reason.
Things aren't always going to look pretty, or feel comfortable, or even seem necessary.
Just have enough faith not to quit.
Understand that things work out how and when they are supposed to.
Use everything that happens to you and around you as tools to help build.
The good and the bad but serve a greater purpose.
Don't allow temporary circumstances to cloud your vision.
Realize that the testing of your faith is to produce patience, and
The power in patience gives us the will to persevere, and
Perseverance promises us not just success, but also peace and joy.
Don't run from the struggle; it's there to make you stronger.
Don't be moved by fear because your faith can take you beyond it.

PEACEKEEPERS

Rare to find one who brings more peace than problems, but
If you do, keep them close.
When you are a good person and a natural giver,
The world will try to take as much as they can from you.
Find somebody who's more committed to helping you lift the burdens than adding to them.

DIRECTION

We are all on a journey.
You can be inspired, motivated, and working diligently towards your goals.
However, without direction
The most you will be is busy, but rarely productive.
It's not just about having a dream.
It's about having a plan
And understanding that your choices either contribute to, or constrict, your success.
Be wise.

Rob Hill Sr.

EVIDENCE

The pain is present and burning in my eyes.
Confusion settles in and depression knocks on my door.
I don't answer— I never answer, feelings aren't welcome here.
Emotions left a long time ago.
Is anything ever enough anymore?
Why do I reek of loneliness in a room full of people?
Why do I long for you when you only longed for him?
I can't deny my feelings, but it's evident that...
The pain is present and burning in my heart.
I am told that things will come and go,
And life has proven this to be fact.
The happiness comes in the blink of an eye
But the pain takes forever to go.
As much as I ignore it, as much as I run from it,
The pain sharpens at the sight of you.
Eye contact brings visions of you and him together
And when you're gone, I can't escape those thoughts.
I got played and it hurts but it's evident that...

The pain is very present and burning in my soul.
I hate cupid and his conniving ways.
Shot me in my heart with an arrow to break my guard down,
Then stab me in the back 30 times harder with his dagger of deception.
My love was unconditional,
My intentions were pure,
My dedications was undeniable,
My passion was true.
But all of me has never been enough for half of you.
The proof is in the evidence.

ONE CHOICE

We are all just one choice away from a completely different life.
Be careful with who you allow in your heart.
Be selective with what you give your time to, and
Be unwavering in your faithful pursuit of your dreams.

FORTITUDE IN THE TRENCHES

Patience pays off… Give it time.
Don't move in haste or panic.
Stay open and be willing to work.
Things will come around.
Your outlook attracts certain outcomes.
It's all about how you choose to see things.
Be careful what you speak over yourself.
Your life will go where your words lead it.

KNOW SACRIFICE, KNOW GROWTH

Know yourself.
You can't make everybody happy every time.
Never apologize for believing in yourself enough to sacrifice parts of who you are today
For who you can become tomorrow.

THE ALLURE OF BEAUTY

Beautiful people like her are naturally elusive.
You can never fully have her
Because her spirit was born free and had no intentions of changing.
Her essence was meant to be shared, and experienced,
But on her own terms.
Never to be possessed or controlled by outside standards or expectation.
She is comfortable in her skin, and secure in her own thoughts.
Her being attracted attention but she desired much more than to be seen.
Her appetite was for something bigger than herself.
She was here to teach us how to be present.
She only desired to be loved fully, but never controlled.
She wasn't here to be handled.
And though she was misunderstood by the fearful,
And seen as a bit reckless by the careful,
She still existed, whole and unashamed.
She was free, alive, and full of life in her own world
And it was beautiful to see.

DESIRE VS. VALUE

It's less about how you get what you desire and
More about how you treat what you claim to value—
Effort and appreciation can arrest the heart
After patience and thoughtfulness consume the mind.

WHEN SOON IS TOO FAR

I used to get so frustrated when people would hit me with the
"Your time is coming soon" line.

That's all I used to hear…
My time for love, my time for success, my time for it all
Is "coming soon"… or so they say.

People like to make it seem like if we just wait long enough, everything we want will suddenly appear.
Wait for what's right, wait for who's right, wait for the time to be right.
I get that patience is a priceless virtue, but I need something that pays off.

Because, right now, for me,
"Soon" is just too far away.
I need it here, now… today!

I used to wonder if it ever gets easier.
Maybe it does, or maybe we just get stronger.
Maybe soon comes before we know it but doesn't look the way we imagined it.
Are we looking for better tomorrows but not investing in today?
Maybe we're waiting for something God never intended for us to have
Or maybe He's waiting to see if we'll finally fight for what we deserve.

Maybe we just needed some time to learn how to value our growth.
I say maybe, but in reality, I'm sure.
I know that the experiences and lessons we learn through our mistakes

Are necessary for our success.
But something about the word "maybe" keeps people aware that there's a choice in at all.
We decide each day and with each choice the life we are going to live.

I know the successful have a humbling mastery of these four things:
Faith, initiative, discipline, and love.
We should build all we do on those pillars.
We work and get it done. It's who we are. It's what we do.

And maybe we don't do it all perfectly,
But we can all choose to commit towards making sure
Each one of us consistently gets better.

I know… I know… You're just tired of waiting on your time to come.
You've worked and worked. But realize that's what it takes to get where you're going.
Learn to be okay with everything you have now.
You have enough time and money, now start investing your energy into your ideas.
Learn to embrace your life for what it is, and not what others think it should be.
Focus on making yourself better.

I no longer live for "soon."
I realize that it may never come quite fast enough,
But progress occurs and struggles do subside.
We are alive and blessed beyond measure now.
And that is more than enough for anybody who's truly committed to going somewhere.
When you aren't enough for you or confident in your ability to choose what's best for you,
Soon will always be too far away.

WE JUST WANT A TEAMMATE

Last night you reminded me of why you chose to love me.
You said it was something about how
I was one of the first people to show you I cared for you.
Beyond just what I could get from you,
You enjoyed the chance to be heard without judgement,
To be admired and understood.
You'd never been romanced before.
You just wanted to know what it felt like to get lost in the night
With somebody you could trust to make your happiness a priority.
You wanted to know what it was like
To have the kind of conversations that made you forget to look at your phone.
You wanted to feel like our time truly mattered.
You just wanted to feel like your presence was worthy of a plan.
And maybe not every time,
But certainly often enough to show the effort a woman like you could inspire.
We never forget the ones who are good to us.
The ones who didn't just give up,
The ones who cared enough to teach us something new,
Even after we've disappointed them.
And for me, that person has always been you.
You have always been the one who saw progress.
And you didn't quit on my potential when you got frustrated with my mistakes.
It is because of you that I know good love both challenges our old ways and
Gives us room to grow into better ones.
Knowing you still chose to love me,

Even as I learned how to be me,
Makes me want to work harder for us.
I've decided not to be one of those people who always waits for next time.
I know most say if you love something you let it go
But you have showed me a truth that I can't deny,
And that is, if you truly love something you treat it right.
You showed me that if I wasn't working to keep it
Then I was asking to lose it.
There is no in between.
You're proof that special girls deserve an extraordinary forever,
And I just wanted to take this moment to remind you
That I'm planning for us to spend that forever together.

SOMEBODY TO WIN WITH

It was something about the way they cared for one another
That brought feelings of acceptance.
She just wanted to understand him, not change him.
She just wanted to be part of whatever lifted the burdens, and her actions made that clear.
He knew she could use another reason to smile,
And he decided to be one.
It was refreshing for them
Because they knew the value of each other's time,
They didn't play about business—both had a passion for building.
There was no time to waste trying to force things.
She knew he had options,
And she was confident in her ability to show that she was the best one.
He knew she wasn't hiding behind fear and living under the cloud of being hurt like the rest.
She was open to possibilities but patient.
He was ready to lead but selective.
They valued when things happened naturally.
And it was just something about her smile that made him daydream about their future.
She knew what she wanted, and she was working on herself until she got it.
And he admired her for that.
So, this time, he was determined not get in his own way.
I guess you can say she inspired him.
And sure, he'd been cared for but never really felt invested in, so this was all new for him.
She was different, and they say the truly great ones are always different.
He knew it.
Her being a part of his peace made her a priority for his time.

Hope For Love

They were building one of those bonds that made even the pessimist believers.
And they knew it didn't have to be perfect to be special.
He was on her team and she was his biggest fan.
They just wanted to win together.

TO FEEL REAL LOVE

I just want to feel real love,
Whatever it is,
Whatever it consists of,
Whatever it makes you do,
I want it… because the stuff I've been dealing with just can't be it.

The arguing, the pretending, the blaming,
I'm just done with it.
I used to dream all the time about my happily ever after—
What she would be like,
The places we would go,
The things we would do.
I used to be so excited about my future with her,
But I'm exhausted looking for her.

It's just crazy how the one I'm with rarely ever acts like kind of partner I want.
I try to convince myself that my next partner will be different all the others who fell short
Yet in the end I'm the one who is left different,
Wishing I never tried with some people.
Funny how you can't stop yourself from remembering the disappointments.
You know…
The ones who made you remember them
But for all the wrong reasons.

We never really let those situations go, huh?
Sure, we move along,
But is that the same as moving on?

It's just crazy how the one you want rarely ever acts like what you want.

Hope For Love

Yet, in the end,
I still want to feel real love,
Whatever it is,
Whatever it consists of,
Whatever it makes you do,
I want it… because the stuff I've been dealing with just can't be it.
It just can't be…

REMEMBER HOW WE WERE?

Remember how we were before?
When we didn't care…

Not that we didn't care at all… because we did, and intensely.
But remember how we were before?
When all the things we cared about were simple.

I could like you and solely focus on finding new ways to make you smile.
I could look at you and instantly think of ways to spend our future together.
I could be at a peace in your presence.
You were my escape…
But it's almost as if everything is a facade until feelings get involved.
It's like you talk and you have great moments, but they aren't real.
You spend time together and make memories but once the feelings are too deep to control,
Those times just drift further and further away.

I miss not having to care about your phone or its content.
I miss not having to wonder if you thought of me.
I miss not having to think twice when it came to us.
And it's not because I changed, or you did…
It's not because we were so wrong and naive in the beginning,
Because we weren't.
This is real.
And you know,
Asking you if you remember how we were before made me realize something,
We don't need things to go back to how they were.

Those moments are reserved for that time and that space.

We shouldn't need yesterday back just to appreciate today.
We don't need to get things back to how they used to be.
We need to focus on how we can get past where we are.
We need to work towards reaching where we want to be.
Sure, we had good times… but I believe those were just the start.
We'll get past our troubles and move on to better days.
Forget how good we were before.
How great can we be today?

I'm focused on what this bond can be.
I'm committed to growth
And I'm praying you are too,
Because I ain't letting you go.

YOUR PATH

Your story,
Your testimony,
Your life,
It all has more value than you know.
We were not put here to be islands.
We were put here to be blessings.
Greatness isn't something God only gives to a select few.
Greatness is in all of us.
Unfortunately, it's only cultivated by some of us.
You are still alive
And well enough to read these words for a reason.
Whatever happened to you didn't kill you.
It may have hurt but it wasn't strong enough to break you, so
Don't allow it to stop you from moving forward.
You are more than your pain.
You are more than your heartbreaks and your mistakes.
Your mission on this earth is not just to survive,
Your mission is to thrive.
Don't let the world intimidate you, and get you to believe that
You are behind.
You are not behind. In fact, you are exactly where you should be.
Today, this very moment is the perfect opportunity to make dreams come true.

MAMA SAID SO

Mama said "Son, keep going."
I guess she saw me about to stop.
I went from feeling like a quitter

To acting like one.
Yeah, no guessing involved.
I needed that reminder.

Because it's so easy to forget how beautiful we are as we develop.
It's easy to forget that we are masterful works in progress.
That we aren't going to have it all together
And that we aren't even supposed to.
I used to say things about my past like,
"Back when I was living wrong,"
As if it was necessary to shame who I was
In hopes that it would make who I am appear
Better, if possible.

In reality though, I wasn't living "wrong,"
I was just living what I knew.
I was inexperienced and everything I did is what you do when you're inexperienced—
You make mistakes and bad choices.

And some things we learn the first time.
Other lessons we need repeatedly to fully grasp
Without beating ourselves up for learning,
Because that's all we're essentially doing
Even though that's not what we tell ourselves.

But...
Mama said, "Son, keep going."

I guess she respected how far I'd come
And she recognized how far I could go,
And I appreciate her for that little boost.
I needed it.
Not because I was about to quit, but because it enriched my perspective.

I wasn't wrong, I was growing.
And I was doing it the best way I knew how.
So, every time I'm low and I feel like letting up
I just remember those words. I just remember to keep going.
And if for no other reason I do it because my mama said so!

DADDY STOPPED DREAMING

Daddy said he stopped dreaming a long time ago.
Said something about not having time to.
I didn't really get it so I asked a few questions,
And surprisingly, he had a few answers.

He started off by telling me the window for his dream had already passed him.
Said he could've did this and could've did that but…
There was always a "but" with him.
It was usually my cue to stop listening.

Why did I have to have the daddy who stopped dreaming?
He told me things like
Work hard,
Fight for what you want,
Always have a plan.
But those are hard to hear when you don't even understand
How Daddy stopped dreaming.

He said something about bills and debt.
It was always something about bills and debt…
The kind of something that made me feel like that's all I'd grow up to.
It made me feel like all I'd do was pay bills and die,
Especially if I missed my window to dream.

But I struggled to accept that reality.
I couldn't.
In fact, I realized that if there's ever a reality too painful for me to accept
Then it is my responsibility to change
Either myself or that reality.

You see, daddy said he stopped dreaming,
But what he didn't realize is that he had a child yearning for his example.
And when you have a child you never stop dreaming… ever!
Because you know that kid is going to base a large part of whether their dreams Are realistic or not off of what you did or didn't do with yours.

But then again, that wasn't my daddy's problem.
He had bills and debt to worry about.
My life was mine and I had to make something out of it.
So even though it's been years since daddy stopped dreaming,
I go twice as hard for mine… And my son is the reason!

FOREVER LOVE

Today marks 10 years of fatherhood,
10 years of growth,
10 broken generational curses,
10 years of hope.
Here's to 10 decades with you son,
10 generations of love,
10 acres for legacy,
10 friends to trust,
And, 10 prayers you stay patient
And the final 10 is a statement:
Believe in yourself, don't ever doubt that you'll make it.

UP

Mixed emotions when it's time to open… up.
You try and you try to talk but the words just won't come… up.
You feel yourself slipping, and slipping, and you just want to sit… up.
You want to feel… up.
You're tired of… down.
But it seems that with you, it always comes… down.
It comes down to you falling short,
Dropping the ball,
Missing the cue,
Being used,
Feeling stuck,
But… you just want to be… up.
You just want your family good,
Bills paid,
Options open,
Love flowing,
Laughter everywhere,

You… just want to be… up.
And it's hard when you just don't know how to get there.
And though there's a lot of different paths for each journey,
You just pray the one you're on somehow leads you… up.
Because that's all we want to be…
We just want to be… up.
And free.
And happy.
And in love.
And successful.
And away from anything that can interrupt that.
I think it's time to go… up.

DO YOU WANT TO BE HAPPY?

I was asked if I wanted to be happy
And I didn't have an answer for them because
The question seemed juvenile…
I mean…
Of course, I want to be happy.
Doesn't everybody?
Don't we all want joy, love, laughter, peace of mind, and
Well…
Happiness?

I guess the cold reality of it is...
Not everybody wants to be happy.
And that's the reason for the question.
Some people have been hurt so much that "damaged" is all they know how to be.
Pain is all they know how to feel.
Everything outside of it just makes them uncomfortable.
Maybe I was becoming this person and
That's why I was asked the question,
"Do you want to be happy?"
Well… I do… I mean I did…
Nah…
I do want to be happy.
I deserve to be happy, so…
It's time I work towards making me happy.

Even if its uncomfortable,
Even if it requires more than I have learned how to give,
Even if it means change at all cost,
I. Want. To. Be. Happy.

And I want the way I look, live, and love to make that so clear
That I'm never asked that question again.

DEAR CHANEL

I really don't know what it is with you, I just know that I love you.
Seeing all you've been through, the struggles, the disappointment, the pain,
I just wanted to be the one who finally fought for you.
I know you were used to being played and cheated.
I know you were used being judged and hated.
I know you were used to being lonely and independent.
But for the life of me, all I wanted you to be used to was my love.
I wanted you to be used to being called beautiful in the morning.
And hearing "I love you" in the evenings.
I wanted you to be used to having somebody to depend on,
And being confident in knowing you had a lover who didn't want to leave you.
I wanted you to be used to somebody investing in your smile
And committing to being one of the best parts of your future.
I wanted you to be used to me
Loving you.
You shared so much with me.
I knew about your mom, your dad, your brothers and sisters
I knew about all the moving and the fighting.
I knew about the deaths and how it hurt you to lose your grandfather.

I knew about it all and I just wanted to be the one
Who made every one of your disappointments feel like a blessing in disguise.
Because you reminded me a lot of myself. We are fighters by nature.
We fight to prove we are right, to prove we don't care, to prove we are tough.
Whatever the case may be, we just fight.
And when you are a fighter it's so hard to let anybody close.
It's so hard to trust, to receive, to care because
You just never know if it will be worth the energy.
But perhaps one of the worst parts about being a fighter in our case is
The fear of not being enough.
The fear of giving everything and losing myself.
And each day with you, that was my fear.
And it kept me from committing.
You didn't deserve half, but I wasn't whole.
I gave what I could until things got old.
But don't think for one second that loving you from a distance is easy.
I still check up on you, I just observe and watch from the background.
I loved that outfit when you went out, and that new hair color is perfect.
It's just unfortunate that my pride wouldn't allow me to let you know.
Maybe I failed you, maybe I didn't.
You say you still have love for me
And that's all I can really ask for after all we've been through.
You've always been special to me
And I'll always wish the best for you,
My dearest, Chanel.

SOLID GROUND

Where is solid ground?
On what street is everything okay?
I need the address to Right.
You know, "getting it right,"
Or, "we gon' be alright."
You know, living the right way?
Do you have it?
I need the address to Forever…
My relationships can't seem to find it.
I always get lost at the intersection of Sacrifice and Unconditional.
Maybe it's the construction, but it always feels different.
I can't see it with my GPS.
Can you guide me?
I will settle for the address to Peace.
I will settle for a break.
And not a heartbreak or breakup,
But a breakthrough, a breaking down the barriers.
You know, like breaking the mold,
Being free,
And feeling home.

THE PROCESS

Faith gave me peace,
Failure gave me strength,
Losing gave me foresight,
Forgiveness gave me healing.
Rejection gave me determination,
Struggle gave me drive,
Discipline gave me opportunity,
Purpose gave me value.
Experience gave me wisdom,
Love gave me joy.

PART THREE

LOST IN SEPTEMBER

Facing my fear.
Finding my purpose.
Feeling more worthy.

MY WHY

I guess before, I didn't really know what I was living for.
There was no why, no purpose, no real reason.
I'd just wake up and do whatever, because I guess that's just what people with no "why" do.

But they say, "What wisdom cannot teach, rock bottom can."
And when you're at the bottom,
And you know you're there because of your own choices
You start waking up fast.

You start asking questions like,
Why am I here?
What am I living for?
What's my purpose?

And I guess for me it finally clicked.

I'm here on purpose; this is all by design.
Life isn't perfect but it's getting better because I keep working.
I know why I'm here.
I know what I'm living for.
I know what my purpose is.
I found my "why."
And I'll live for it
Until the day I die.

THE DREAMERS NIGHTMARE

How do you balance putting all of your heart into something
But still make time to give it to someone?
Being a dreamer, I always feel torn.

You want the love and the success
But while you're pursuing one, it seems like the other is getting away from you.
Of course, you want to balance them both.
The whole "you make time for what you want" theory is accurate.
And while I agree, thoughts of chasing the wrong thing can be scary.

I want to be able to build my business and make you happy as my partner.
I want to be able to focus on my dreams and still make you feel like a part of them.
I want you to see that pursuing my purpose over here
Isn't taking away from my passion for you.
But... it seems like you don't get it.
When I'm locked in and working, you think I'm closing you out.
When I talk about growing you think it means apart from you.
I try to explain but you don't get it.
It's like, you'd rather me forget it.

You told me, "Don't follow your heart if it's going to lead you away from me."
It hurt... because I'd never ask you to wait for me.

It's like I'm feeling stuck...
If the one you love was handing you their heart,
But life was handing you your dreams,

Which would you grab?

Ideally, you'd want to have both.
And they say you shouldn't have to choose.
But sometimes it really feels like you do.

You want it all but it's hard when everything has its own timing.
And respecting that sometimes feels like a long waiting game.
This journey is rough.

I just pray I find somebody who consistently helps me enjoy it.

WHEN I FALL AGAIN

When I fall in love again, I'll know it was by choice.
I'll know it was because I searched for and it found me.
And I'll know that I chose to receive it.

If by chance my relationship fails,
I don't want to be the person that hates love.
I want to take accountability for the things I could've done better.

I want to acknowledge those times where I could have compromised but didn't.
Where I could have given but didn't.
And where I should have listened but didn't.
I don't want to be the person who forever blames love for my shortcomings.
I don't want her to be the girl who turns bitter because I couldn't love her better.

Hope For Love

I don't want us to be the ones who gave up when it was time to put work in.

I want to be real and realize that love isn't responsible when I spoke in anger,
Or the times I lashed out in revenge and spite,
Or even the painful times I've blindfolded myself from the truth with fear.
I want to be the person who acknowledged their imperfections,
Who accepted their wrongs and weaknesses,
But knew that love was still just as perfect as God designed it to be.
I want my partner to understand that we complicated things.
We ran from chances.
We made mistakes.

I want it to be understood that we tried our best.
I want her to know that we loved and learned.
And that we don't fall short just because we loved and lost.

I want it to be known that we chose to give pieces of ourselves that were priceless.
We chose compassion, understanding, and trust
Over fear, doubts, and insecurities.

I want us to know that we did what real lovers do.
I want to trust that even though we didn't give perfectly, we still gave our all.
I want to believe we kissed before goodnights and said I love you before goodbyes.

More than anything I want us to have faith
That as long as we're still breathing,
We'll live to love another day.

MAYBE WE CAN BUILD

I have to be inspired by you.
I have to see something in you that makes me want more for us.
I'll never be content with bare minimum love.
I need that overflowing, ever fulfilling type of bond.
I'm attracted to passion and direction.
I need a person who has the same appreciation for accomplishment that I have.
So…

I want to see you grinding.
I want to see your eyes light up when you start talking about your passion.
I want to be there, building towards my own dreams
But supporting you while you lay the foundation for yours.
And then I want us to come together
And I want us to build the type of bond people daydream about.
I want us to connect in a way that allows us to grow in every way.
New heights for your career and different levels for me in mine.

A couple that can't motivate each other has a relationship with an expiration date,
And that can't be us.
When I'm off track, you'll keep me focused.
When you're down, I'm in your ear reassuring you of your greatness.

And I'm not saying it'll be easy because no journey is perfect.
But…
If you stick it out with me,

Hope For Love

I promise to spend the rest of my life making sure you know it was worth it.

And I'm not sure where your heart is with all this,
But if we're on the same page,
Maybe we can build.

TRYING TO GET IT RIGHT

I'm starting to feel like I'm the only one who's looking for love.
And maybe I'm looking too hard,
Or maybe I'm thinking too much,
But I'm just trying to get it right, trying to find the one.

Crazy how its perceived as corny or even weak
To actually care about somebody these days.
Since when is wanting something real and lasting dumb?
Whether its popular to admit or not, we all long for that connection and the opportunity to Be with somebody we don't have to hide from.

No matter how much we say we don't care, or how often we get hurt, or how little things change, we all secretly have hope for love.
We all hope the next time will end differently than the last time and the key is letting go of the past and the fears.

But…

I'm starting to feel like I'm the only one who's looking for love.
And maybe I'm looking too hard,
Or maybe I'm thinking too much,
But I'm just trying to get it right, trying to find the one.

You see…
The beauty of the possibilities is simple.
It's having something to look forward to even when you swore you were done looking.

Hope For Love

And though the picture isn't as clear as I want it be today, my heart is too big not to have Hope for tomorrow.
I'm not saying I'm trying to force it.
I'm just saying I know it's worth it.
Even if that means getting hurt a few times.

Because more than anything,
I'm just trying to get it right with somebody
Who's just as tired of getting it wrong as I am.

I HAD A DREAM

I had a dream I could change you.
Not just because I could make you into who I wanted you to be,
But because I finally got to see you as the "you" I always knew you could be.

In my dream, all the potential turned into promise.
I didn't have to motivate you because you were already motivated.
I didn't have to teach you because you were so eager to learn, that you were always ahead.

I had a dream I could change you,
And that's exactly what I did.
I changed you
For us.

I had a dream I could change you.
I took your weaknesses and I strengthened them.
I changed the parts of your body that you didn't like, and made you love them.
That way I wouldn't have to hear you complain about flaws I saw nothing but beauty in.

In my dream, the insecurities turned into confidence.
I told you that you were beautiful, and you actually believed me.
I told you that I loved you and you didn't question it.
See, I had a dream that I could change you,
And that's exactly what I did.
I changed you
For us.

I had a dream I could change you.

Hope For Love

I took away all your fears and I replaced them with courage.
I took away all the trust issues and I replaced them with faith.

In my dream, the doubts turned into desires.
You stopped caring about getting hurt and you started wondering how to accept love.
You stopped questioning and you started believing.
I gave you an outlook on life that allowed you to let me in.

See, I had a dream I could change you,
And that's exactly what I did.
I changed you
For us.

I had a dream I could change you.
But I woke up without you.
I changed you into a person that you couldn't recognize.
Somebody you were scared to see.
A version of you, that you just weren't ready to be.

In my dream, it all seemed so simple.
But in changing you,
It allowed me to see
It's pointless settling for a person I'll only ever meet in my dreams.

So instead of changing you,
I had to change how I felt about you.
And move on…
For me!

MIRRORS

The mirrors at your house always seem to get foggy when I'm trying to find myself.
I see remnants of you in too many of my bad decisions.
Do all the lessons you teach involve pain?
If so, I'm not that kind of student.
We fell in love to be free.
I won't learn to be less of me just to make room for you.
Growth is my only aim,
And mutual love would only make more room for that.
Your presence didn't always make me feel out of place
But I breathe differently around you now.
And I used to swear love could only live at your house.
That's until I looked in my own mirror and saw me without the fog.
I would say I don't look like what I have been through, but that would be a lie.
I look like every day of my life mattered because that is what I believe.
I don't regret one time I came over to your house, but I won't be back.
I will lock the door on my way out.

WHAT I MISS MOST

I miss having something to look forward to.
I miss having conversations you never want to end,
moments you never want to forget,
And laughs that never seem to stop.
I miss the talks
And the time spent together.

I miss that time when I stopped and reflected
On the fact that I never imagined you meaning so much to me.

I miss that day when I looked at you and felt invincible.
I miss that time when I was doubting everything
And you made me feel like I could handle anything.
I miss the beginning.
I miss the potential.
I miss the possibilities.

I miss what I dreamed we would be.
I miss what I prayed we would share.
I miss what I thought we were.

I miss the idea of us.

EVEN IF YOU

Even if you could love her right,
Like even if you could be the reason she smiled,
Or the consistency she needed, or the support she was missing…
The most her fears would ever allow you to be is "too good to be true."

Because to her, the memory of that pain
Is more important than opportunities and possibilities.

She's taken chances before and she doesn't have the time to see if you're different…
Because even if you're incredible, she'll only see your flaws,
And even if you're genuine she'll only see your mistakes.

It's easier to complain than it is to change, so no matter how great you are,
It's just easier to be scared than it is to step up.
And she's comfortable… she's having fun.
Her friends told her she has time, there's no rush to find the one.
She's living, she's not trying to waste time dealing with feelings.
So even if you're what she needs,
She's just not ready for the work right now.
And like it or not, that's just what you have to deal with
When you're dealing with a heart that you didn't break.

So, if you aren't patient and prepared for the long ride, just quit while you're ahead.

Because all she trusts is the game.
And by the time you climb that wall,
She'll have already moved her heart behind a taller one.

NO REGRETS

Looking back, I guess it's easy to see all the things I could've done differently.
The listening, the compromising, the sacrificing.

I could've done a lot more to keep you
But at the time, my only focus was protecting me.
But can you blame me?
When you're always the one being quit on,
You start to question if anything is worth fighting for.

The reality is, you could be this genuinely incredible person and still be overlooked
Because people don't want something real anymore.
They just want reasons to complain and excuses to avoid.

Having a good thing is so hard because meeting a strong person is so rare.
So, I've learned to respect when people run from me.
I realize my kind of love ain't for everybody
And I'm at peace with that.

I have no regrets.

KEEP ON KEEPING ON

Keep going.
Keep loving.
Keep your head up.
Keep your mind open.
Keep giving.
Keep learning.
Keep getting better.

GENERATIONAL DREAMS

Coming up they told me boys that look like me would end up either dead or in jail.
They never really gave my type a shot,
But then I saw Barack make it to the top.
And then I started thinking, and dreaming for more
Thoughts like, "I can make sure the grandkids of my grandkids are financially set forever."
I could turn "dead or in jail" to "alive and well."
I could be the hope for my people.

It's a generational dream…
The kind of thoughts that drive great men to change things.

I was scared to be a father; I didn't think I could raise a boy to be a man.
I was still learning my own way out of boyhood…
You know, still trying to figure things out.
I was still fighting the shadow of my absent father,
Promising myself that I'd try harder
To be better man, a better role model… to be a better friend.

Hope For Love

I know it's not in every man to be a leader of men
But I was just dreaming for an opportunity to do things better than him.
Cause coming up all I ever heard was that boys like me end up dead or in jail.
They never really gave my type a shot,
But then I saw Jay-Z make it to the top.

And then I started thinking, and dreaming for more
Thoughts like, "I can make sure the grandkids of my grandkids are good forever"
I could turn "dead or in jail" to "alive and well."
I could be the hope for my people.

It's a generational dream...
The kind of thoughts that drive great men to change things.

So, I don't really care what they have to say about boys like me now.
I don't care about what my Pops did or did not do.
I don't care that they weren't willing to give my type a shot.
I don't care about anything but making things better for my young king.
Because what I see for him, is much better than the little they saw for me.

It's a generational dream...
The kind of thoughts that drive great men to change things.
And that's just what I plan to do.

FIVE YEAR FEARS

I don't want to be "here" in five years.

I want to believe that the work I'm doing is leading me somewhere
I'd like to be in a position to look back…
And laugh at all the times I thought I was off track

I know there's no perfect science to this life stuff
There's no always getting it right…
No shortcut to happily ever after…
No spotless path to success

But I just don't want to be "here" in five years

I want to believe that all the sacrificing and patience will pay off
I'd like to be in a place to think back…
And laugh at all the times I thought I was off track
It's just the waiting that kills me
It's the being ambitious but having to respect the process
The living and the learning, but realizing that I'll never know enough

But I do know one thing…
I know there's no perfect science to this life stuff
So, as I think about the next five years, I just pray that I don't live them in fear
I pray I try new things and connect with different people
I pray I visit foreign places and do away with my comfort zone
I pray for the courage to step up and live…
Where others would step back and miss out

I pray for the opportunity to live these dreams…
And accomplish all the things God has for me in this lifetime

And I know if I trust His will, and stay consistent in the midst of these fears,
The last place I'll be…
Is "here"
In 5 years

FOR THE TEARS YOU WON'T CRY

I wonder why you fear yourself,
Why you ignore your heart,
And why you suppress your soul.
What are you so scared of?

Who told you that you shouldn't love yourself?
Or that you didn't deserve the best?
Who said you had to be comfortable feeling miserable?

Is it life?

How is it that I can see the world in your eyes, but you can't?
How is it that I can hear the song in your spirit, but you don't?
How is it that I can feel the restless rumblings in your heart, but you deny them?

Is it love?
You gave your all and never got it back?
You played the fool and lost your sense of self?
You tried and tried but you always came up short?

What are you so scared of?
Is it rejection?

You hear your heart crying, but you're afraid to listen.
You tell yourself lies that you refuse to mention.
Why is it so hard for you to be truthful with yourself?

Is it fear?

You doubt your own strength, but you've survived being hurt before.

You run from everything that's good for you, but the pain is getting hard to ignore.
You're on the pursuit of happiness but why haven't you started looking for it within?
Is it pain?

That feeling of falling in love but knowing you could land in regrets?
That chance at having a good thing and not knowing what to expect?
You play hard to get, but you're really just scared to give.

And so, I ask…
What are you so scared of?
Is it you?

MY APOLOGIES

I guess I thought you'd be a little happier for me
Seeing as though I kept going, kept fighting, kept striving for more.
I know what we used to do… I remember how things used to be.
But I'm just not there anymore.

When we talked about wanting it all, I really meant that.
When we talked about being great, I really felt I deserved that.
When we talked about making history, I really wanted to do that.

But I'm sorry…
All you see is that I've changed…
But that's half the story.

I guess I thought we'd pick things up again at some point.
I thought maybe it was growing pains and we'd eventually see eye to eye again.
You know,
The "if you love it let it go and if it comes back you know it's yours" type of thing.
But we never could get it back to what it was.

When we talked about forever, I meant that.
When we talked about never taking things for granted, I saw that.
When we talked about always staying true, I felt that.

But I'm sorry.
You say I'm not the same…
When you're growing, you can't help but change.

I guess I thought it would all turn out differently.
You chase a dream and the closer you get to it the faster things change.
Family isn't as familiar, friends act worse than strangers,
And the loyalty becomes a matter of convenience.

I've just realized I can't live life trying to fit in the boxes people constantly build for me.
And if I've ever disappointed you,
My apologies.

I WISH YOU WELL

You never really cared like you said you did.
I can see it now.
I used to be angry about it, reflecting on how much I put into it.
The dates, the trips, the conversations…
The feelings…
I wanted it all back, but you know how that goes.

You never get it back; you just learn to move on.
Because once the respect is lost, the relationship is over,
Regardless of who did who wrong.

But I realize I had to go through that to get where I am today.
Going through it hurt but it brought me something better.

And now…
I'm thinking about the last time I thought about you
I thank God that I'm on to something new.

Something where the good is reciprocated not underappreciated.
Something that see's my potential and cares enough to invest in it.
Something that loves past flaws and believes in working through mistakes.
Something real, not something perfect.
It's something better,
And I deserve it.

Regardless of whether it works out
Or whether I get hurt again,
Or whether I'm lied to, cheated on, whatever…

What I learned from you, was that every time I'm broken, I can choose to get better.
I can choose to forgive.
I can choose to move on.
I can choose to get stronger.
I can choose to be happy and I don't have to be cold.

Because whether you really cared like you said you did or not,
It's all in the past and I'm better because of the experience.

And now...
I'm sitting back thinking about the last time I thought about you
I thank God that I'm on to something new.
And even though at the time what we had felt like hell
The best in me still wishes you well.

Rob Hill Sr.

WE COULD HAVE THAT

You know those happily ever after stories…
The ones where the couple goes through hell,
But somehow make it out against all the odds?
They sort through the problems and deal with the issues
But they do it together…

And it seems like they work things out without ever having to question if it's all worth it…

You know when you see an older couple…
They're holding hands and conversing…
And you sit there wondering how they still have anything to talk about after all these years…
You come up with this story about how they almost lost it all
He was laid off from his job, but she stuck with him…
Or she had cancer but he held her down every step of the way…

I catch myself wondering if it all exists anymore.
You know…
The "I don't care what comes up, we're going to get through it" type of situations.
The "I'm not concerned with your past, let's build this future" type of connections.
The "I'm committed to protecting your heart
With the same passion I used to guard my own" type of love.
I see that…
And maybe I'm crazy…
But I believe we could have that
If we want it bad enough.

WHEN LOVE LEAVES

Damn shame that when
Love leaves the heart,
Life leaves the man.

WHAT I WANT

I want to keep up,
I want you to love,
I want to stay true,
I want us to trust.

IF NOT US, THEN WHO?

It's on people like us to live in a way that keeps the world encouraged.
It's on people like us to be the reason the next person doesn't give up.

The question isn't "why us?", the question is "why not us?".
We were put here to change things.
We were put here to shake the world up.
That's why normal just isn't appealing to us.
We're here to be historic, remembered, and celebrated…
And if not us,
Then who?

TOO TIRED FOR FITNESS

Not again, not anymore.
There was no more to gain from being close.
Not a NYC, DC, or LA…
Just more of all the wrong things.
Some felt good, others felt forced, but each time
I came back wanting to see if anything changed,
Hoping you saw me.
Always leaving with a little less than before.
How come every time we do this again you're the only one that gains?
We promised each other full support.
I drop it all when you need me to hold you up.
Why does lifting your spirits leave me crushed?
We should get better in some way every time we do this,
But I feel like my gains aren't matching the reps I'm putting in.
Weight too heavy, plates unbalanced, I could be lifting wrong.
Fear and worry, effort slacking.
Still, too tired to move on.

I HOPE WE FIND A WAY

I've gotten this life thing wrong a lot.
I don't date perfectly,
And I haven't always known how to love unconditionally.

I guess I used to think the stars would align
And I'd just end up with somebody who understood me.

You know…
The type of person who knows how to get through to you.
Somebody who knows you well enough to challenge you when you need it,
Who'll pray with you when you feel defeated.
One who knows how to back up and be your peace when times get heated.
And I realize that there's no perfect relationship.
Every conversation won't be full of laughter.
And every moment won't feel like bliss.
I get all of this…

But maybe my problem is I want something that's easy to fight for.
I want something so fulfilling that I never have to think twice about quitting.
I want a love so rewarding that I never consider going back to life without it.
I want a relationship so valuable that I confidently ignore my fears
When they try to bring doubts in it.
But I don't want it bad enough to force it.
I want it right, so I'm willing to wait.
And in the meantime, I'm just working on me.
In hopes that we'll find a way
To our forever.

PART FOUR

LOVED BY DECEMBER

Releasing false expectations.
Forgiving myself.
Ready for love.

WHO ARE WE?

Who are we not to make history?
Who are we not to be moguls, geniuses, and visionaries?
Who are we not to want it all and to be audacious enough to believe we deserve it?
Who are we not to be timeless and celebrated?
Who are we not to redefine the standard?

Who says we have to be "normal."

None of us were born to be normal. Mediocrity is a choice just as greatness is.
You can't force anybody to be great or to live up to their potential.
But who are we not to chase our dreams?
Who are we not to start our own businesses?
Who are we not to test the limits and boundaries and surpass all expectations?

Who says we have to be "normal?"

None of us were born to be complacent.
We are all here for change.
In each of us there is a unique gift,
Something special for us to leave our unique mark on the world.
Who says we have to dumb it down so people don't feel uncomfortable?
Who says that we aren't supposed to be the movers and the shakers?
Who says that we can't lead and influence thousands to live extraordinary lives?

Hope For Love

Who says we have to be "normal?"

We were all put here for a divine reason.
And there is unlimited power and potential in each one of us.
We aren't here to be swayed by fears and doubts.
We are here to conquer, we are here to flourish, we are here to prosper.

Who says we have to be "normal?"

We are here as signs of God's grace, mercy, and remarkable favor.
We are beautiful, talented, and blessed beyond measure.
And who are we not to be?
We aren't normal.
We are here to be legendary.
We are here to inspire.

But most of all,
We are here to love.

Rob Hill Sr.

LOTTERY

Is it that she is...
Infatuated with his mind?
In love with his demeanor?
Or overwhelmed by his presence?

Her stares reflect her heart.
Her actions reflect true love.
Her being reflects his favor.

Is it that he is...
Engulfed in her confidence?
Overcome by her grace?
Or blessed by her existence?

His eyes scream fear.
His walk embodies his nerves.
His hands sweat at her touch.

Is it is that they are…
Afraid to take on forever,
Too selfish to overcome their past,
Or so stuck in what is now?

Take a chance.
Take a chance.
Take a chance.
It just might work out.
I wonder if it's her.
Or could it be him?
Pressure is on both of them.

She scratched to win.
He picked to play.
It's all on luck at the end of the day.

UNTHINKABLE

I told her, “give me your hand so I can give you my heart.”
She hesitated. She knew she could trust me, and I think that scared her.
She’s been hurt before,
She’s been lied to,
She’s been led to believe that good men willing to take the lead
Only exist in the Bible.
She’s not ready for the unthinkable.
She just thought it would be cool to kick it with me.

She didn’t recognize the feelings I sparked within her.
She knew that life was a long story of things that seemed too good to be true.
You know, the kind of happiness meant for others but never for her.
You know the story of the girl who meets the guy and the fall in love, and
Blah blah blah…
But see she’s been hurt before,
She been lied to,
She’s been led to believe that good men willing to commit
Only exist in the Bible.
She’s not ready for the unthinkable.
She just thought it would be cool to chill with me.

She told me what she deserved.
She said she was too good to settle.
She said that she deserved a real man.
One who would protect her and ride for her, profess his love for her.
She wasn’t looking for a knight in shining armor.
All she wanted was a man with a heart that was focused on her.

So, I said, "give me your hand and I'll give you my heart."
She's been hurt before,
She's been lied to,
She's been led to believe that good men willing to keep it real
Only exist in the Bible.
She's not ready for the unthinkable.
She just thought it would be cool to spend some time with me.

So, I told her exactly how I felt.
I told her that this is exactly everything she deserved to have.
I told her that running was the last thing on my mind,
And that I would work for her love.
I told her that if she cried, I would kiss every single tear,
And if she needed me, I would be right there.
I told her the days of fighting alone were over.
She might not need a knight, but I'd be her soldier.

And sure, she's been hurt before,
And yeah, she's were lied to,
But there's a real man standing beside her now.

So why wait for you fears to catch up?
Why second guess the best feeling you've ever experienced?
Why wait for eventually?
If we're going to do something, we should do it right now.
You say you deserve it. I know you deserve it.
And I will give it to you, if you let me.
So, I was wondering maybe, could I make you my baby?
And if we did the unthinkable, would it make us look crazy?

Or would it be so beautiful… either way I'm saying.
If I ask you,
Are you ready?

TIMELINES

I am learning to get rid of all my "by this age" ideas.
They were all off.
Things happen when they are supposed to and not a minute before.
We make too many timelines for things we have no control over.
We have to stop letting other people dictate how we view and value our lives.
None of us are as perfect as we think we need to be.
False expectations make life more difficult than it has to be.
We say we want a forever thing
But most love like it's just something to do when you're bored.
We have to stop rushing everything,
I'd rather have a person who is prepared to be a partner
Than somebody who is just tired of being lonely.
Trying to force anything with love is the perfect way to sabotage it.

IS THAT TOO MUCH TO ASK?

Be intriguing, be a breath of fresh air, be a heart changer.
Have a certain mystery to yourself.
Don't bore me then expect to get more from me.
Make me wonder. Give me something to fantasize about.
And get me thinking…
Be somebody I can dream with until the end of time.
Or is that too much to ask?
Be a challenge, be an inspiration,
Be consistent and not predictable.
There is nothing fascinating about the usual.
There is nothing desirable about somebody with no imagination.
There is no fun without spontaneity.
Be somebody I can grow with until the end of time,
Or is that too much to ask?

I don't want something normal.
Let's build something incredible by doing everything different.
We will redefine what works, and we will inspire a return to love.
We could be the new definition of happiness.
We won't do anything perfectly, but we will be committed to giving our best.
And we won't quit. We will take it one day at a time.
But we will give each day a piece of us to remember.
Something new and unique. We won't rush things.
We will be patient and let forever take care of itself.

Just be somebody I can pray with.
Until the end of time,
Be somebody who won't quit on my potential when they get frustrated with my mistakes.
Be committed to building a forever. But for now,

Let's just promise to make this something worth remembering.
Is that too much to ask?

Rob Hill Sr.

HOW BOYS LEARN TO LOVE

So, the world told you what a man was
And you believed it.
You saw those guys on the street,
You saw those men your mom dated,
You saw those dudes your sister fell for,
And from that, you figured out what a man was…
So, you thought.
You heard the arguments,
You heard him slap her,
And then you heard her beg him not to go
And from that, you figured out what a man was.
Well at least you figured out what a man was supposed to do.
If nothing, you figured out what a man was supposed to look like
And you imitated that.
You learned your manhood
By replaying those fights in your head.
And you and adapted that dysfunction.
See what you heard them scream was love
But all you felt in those voices was pain.
What they told you were tears of joy
Turned out to be tears of shame.
And what you learned more than anything
Was that love, don't love nobody,
So, you decided to play the game. And what you became
Was the image of man built from the imagination of a boy?

See you never really saw a real man.
All you saw was somebody just as lost as you, but a lot older than you,
Pretending to be something he thought was true.
What you learned was to never cry,
And to never show you cared.

But you didn't learn the reasons why and that left you unprepared.
Nobody told you that so-called strength you had, came from fear, not confidence.
What you didn't learn was a real way to love, you just learned how give compliments.
Love is considered stressful when you don't know how to do it.
When you know how to love it's no longer stress, it's necessary work.
Most men can't relate to the influence of a good woman
Because they are not attracted to women who challenge them.
See boys need that quick fix, that easy loving, that fast slide,
Never understanding that they want it quick because subconsciously
They know they couldn't last past that first ride.

See, you don't know how to love because you barely know how to live.
That applause the young boys get for being reckless
Quickly silences when you're having kids and looking for quiet ways to exit.
That thrill the young men toast to is hardly satisfying
When it's nothing left but bad credit and past due bills to sort through.
See, maybe having a plan was a step you were never exposed to
And that's why the system is so quick to expose you.

See that woman you talk down to has the blood of a queen,
And somehow, she found you…
But she learned her love from a mother who loved men who weren't really men.

And she lost herself staying out in the streets trying to find him.
Take it from me because I've been there.
I've had them all and vowed to love them never,
But then I grew up and I got myself together.
And I can blame my father
But it's not his fault that his father chose to falter,
Leaving three generations to learn love from loveless daughters.
This is how boys learn to love and the reason they never find out the why of love.
They will never understand what they stand to gain because they can't imagine
The impact a real woman can have on the life of a good man.
It's the cycle, so their minds stay frozen
Boys learning from boys, so
How to love, they'll never know.

WHERE YOU FROM?

It's not about where you are from, it's about where you are going.
People only care about where you are from when they can identify with where you are going.
You can talk about where you are from, you can talk about what you used to do,
You can talk about who you used to be with,
But nobody cares until they know where you are going.
Where you are from does not matter until people can see where you are going.
You can be the realist in your neighborhood, you can be the smartest, strongest, and
You can be the boldest, but it does not matter where you are from

Until people can see where you are going.
All that real stuff that you pride yourself on,
All that stuff that you think you do that is cool
It may be cool, but cool ain't gon' to get you to great.
It may be fly, but fly ain't gon' to get you to great.
Until it's real, until it makes somebody feel a certain way,
It ain't gon' to get you to great.

Nobody cares about where you are from.
The only thing that matters is where you are going.
Until you get strong enough to stand for something,
Until you get real enough to be about something,
Until you get true enough to yourself to make people feel a certain way,
You will just be normal.
And nobody normal ever gets remembered.

You can keep reminding people about where you are from,
What you did, and what you are about.
But until people can really connect with you
In a way that makes them feel better about themselves—
Stronger, more confident, more passionate about whatever it is they are doing—
Nobody will care.
Because it's not about where you are from, it's about where you are going.
Nobody wants to know about where you are from
Until they can connect with where you are going.
You can be the realist, congratulations.
You can be the coolest, bravo.
But until you are about something,
Until you are making people feel, and making people better—
Responsible, more accountable, dependable...
Trustworthy, honest, loyal—

If you aren't inspiring people to do any of that
Then you aren't making a difference.
And if you aren't making a difference you won't be able to make a dime
Because nobody cares about where you are from,
The only thing people care about is where you are going.

UNFORTUNATE

She is the type of woman you hate to disappoint.
Not because she expects you to be perfect, but because she trusts you to be real.
It is different when she doesn't even care to play detective.
You are motivated to do better because you know she has faith you will do right.
You want to step up every time because
You know how rare it to have someone
Who is secure enough with themselves to stay around.
And still, at the end of the day,
She is not forcing or asking you to prove anything.
She is only giving you the effort you inspire, not counting favors or faults.
But when the pain begins to visit longer than the pleasure, she is going to change,
And you might not see it coming immediately but you will feel it.
Eventually… reality will set in.
You didn't lose her because she wanted to go.
You lost her because you gave her no reason to stay,
And that's so unfortunate.

MAYBE

Maybe it was never supposed to be what we thought it would be.
Maybe it was supposed to be a few good dinners to fill the lonely nights.
Or maybe it was just supposed to be a sign
That there's still reason to have hope for happiness.
Maybe it was just something that could have been more,
But wasn't meant to be.
Maybe it was never supposed to be a forever kind of thing.
Maybe I was supposed to learn from you so I could prepare for the next.
Maybe I was supposed to see how you changed
So, I could adjust my expectations for future relationships.
Maybe it was something that could have been more,
But wasn't meant to be.

Maybe it was never supposed to be anything more than friendship.
Maybe it was supposed to be a chance for us to enjoy something refreshing and stress free.
Maybe it was supposed to be a chance for us to regroup
And heal from the disappointments of our past.
Maybe it was just something that could have been more,
But wasn't meant to be.

Maybe it was never really going anything more than random fun.
Maybe you weren't really the right one and we forced it to be more.
Maybe you weren't really who you said you were
And I was hiding some parts of me just to keep you.

Hope For Love

Maybe it was just something that could have been more,
But wasn't meant to be.

Sometimes things just don't work out.
Sometimes the season ends before you figure out the reason you began.
Sometimes what you get is less than what it was advertised to be.
And sometimes you just have to accept what you have for what it is
And let go of what you thought it was.
Maybe all the maybes will make up for the mistakes, and maybe they won't.
Maybe they are just there to help us accept the fact that
We had something that could have been more,
But wasn't meant to be.

Rob Hill Sr.

THE MAN I AM

She left me because of you.
See you are the reason good guys finish last.
She left me because you are a coward.
She left me because you didn't think enough of her to stick around.
She left me because you left her…

If you would have taught her love like a real man was supposed to,
Or if you would have taught her consistency, like a real man was supposed to,
Or if you even thought enough of her to tell her she was beautiful,
Like a real man was supposed to,
Then maybe… just maybe…
She wouldn't have left me,
Looking stupid,
Because of you.

She left me because of you.
She told me everything about me was too right,
And therefore, I was too good to be true.
All because of you.
Because you never had the courage to love her mother,
She will never take a chance and love another.
Because you couldn't take care of home,
She thinks every man is a rolling stone.

She left me, because of you.
I have never hated a man I never knew
More than you.
Because she left me, searching for something you stole from her
She left me, looking for something you never showed to her.
And you know what, you sorry excuse for a man,

Hope For Love

She left me with a broken heart.
Not because I couldn't love her,
But because you didn't love her.

It's hard to fill a void in a heart that doesn't know how to be whole.
She left me,
Because you left her.
And now *my* heart
Has turned cold.

SERVICE IS SUCCESS

You have to believe that there is more to life
And you have to be courageous enough to pursue whatever is for you.
You deserve joy, you deserve love, and you deserve peace,
So, you have to do whatever is necessary to protect what's important to you.
Start giving your time to the things that really matter.
All we get is time and choices. That's it.
Appreciate the moments that give your life true value.

This world will never be perfect, but it should be better because you exist.
I believe in the greatness of our hearts and it's time to start healing each other.
Let's show the world a new way.

DEAR LOVE

I have been trying to find the words to say to you.
It's crazy because, what exactly do you say
To the one thing that makes me feel whole
While also making you feel like nothing?
I'm attracted you.
That craving for the smile you bring,
That desire for the warmth of those feelings,
That fire in me burning for happiness…
I miss you Love, I miss you dearly.
Everything changed when you left.
My soul didn't sing the same type of song.
You told me I was hard-headed.
You told me I wouldn't be the same without you.
But I doubted you thinking it was all about me.
I said I would never want you again anyway
Because in the end all you really did was leave.
You grew, you changed, you asked for more.
I was good where we were at.
Our differences led to arguments that eventually led to loneliness.
But I'm back now Love.
I want another shot. I *need* another shot.
The games are over and done now. I promise.
I'm back to square one and it's just me missing you.
I believe in us.
All I'm asking is,
What do I have to do to get you back Love?

BEFORE YOU MISS OUT

Don't overthink yourself out of something special.
Not everything needs to be controlled.
You can't get so busy looking for more that you miss what you're really supposed to see.
If you find a man willing to be honest about his mistakes,
Or a woman strong enough to be secure in her flaws,
Then you have somebody special, somebody worth working with.
You can't be scared to let yourself be happy.
You can't be scared to step up and take a chance.
You can't be scared to care for somebody.
Don't get caught up in looking for perfection because that search will fail you every time.
Stop worrying about things you can't control.
It takes going through some serious trials in life for you to really get what you need.
Without the lies, you wouldn't appreciate the truth.
Without the games, you wouldn't value people with genuine intentions.
Without the test, you wouldn't know your strength.
You can't be scared to let yourself be happy.
You can't be scared to step up and take a chance.
You can't be scared to care for somebody.
Stop justifying the reason you have a wall up and ask God for courage
And discernment, so your heart doesn't have to hide.
Heartbreak is a part of life, not the end of it.
Stop using failed relationships as excuses to be cold, pessimistic, and selfish.
Nothing about love is easy and you are not the only one who has been hurt before.

Hope For Love

There's somebody out there wondering the same things you are,
Feeling those same emotions that you're feeling,
And they are scared, just like you.
So be happy.
Step up and take a chance.
Be strong enough to care for somebody
Before you miss out.

I KNEW A GIRL

I knew a girl once.
And I'd like to think I knew her better than she knew herself.
It was a while ago, but I still knew her.
Just like not like most know her... because I knew more.
I knew more than her sense of humor and her quick wit.
I saw further than her appearance and the front she put up.
I saw past those concealing smiles and forced laughter.
I saw through it all and watched her grow up.

I knew a girl once.
A girl with big dreams and unshakeable faith.
She had a glimmer in her eyes that defined greatness,
A realness in her walk that defied gravity,
A sort of calmness about her spirit that gave you security.
But you wouldn't even know this because I knew more.
I mean, I knew more than the drama surrounding her.
I knew more than the niggas misusing her.
I knew more than the her uninterested "I don't need anybody" facade.
I knew more because I really knew her.
But I guess she was just growing up.

I knew a girl once.
A girl who believed in love but stopped having hope for life.
She became addicted to the pain. I was there as tears raced down her cheeks.
And I watched as her trust was betrayed and her spirit broken.
I spoke truths to her heart.

I listened to her cries.
But you really wouldn't know any of this because I just knew more.
That fear of rejection, that fear of trying, and her fears of disappointment
It's all her, it's all there, it's all real.
She just, won't show it.

I knew a girl once.
Better than she knew herself.
I believed in her, I fought for her, I saw her potential.
I knew more.
I knew the person she desired to be, and
I know the person she decided to be.
That's the girl you know, that's the person you see.
I knew that girl once, but
Now she's a stranger to me.

THE GOOD ONES

People misunderstand what it means to be a good one.
You don't get credit for being honest, loyal, and dependable.
You don't get credit for being trustworthy, consistent, and genuine.
It's appreciated but it's also the standard.
Being a good one means so much more than not giving yourself to someone else.
Can you inspire them to chase their dreams?
Motivate them to apply for a better job?
Add value to their future?
Or patiently help strengthen their weaknesses?
Just because you have good intentions does not mean you're a good one.
Don't expect great rewards for doing the bare minimum.
What you get all depends on what you're willing to give.
It's not just about you, it's not all about them.
It's about give and take…
The more you front, the more fake stuff you will attract.
Start showing what's really in your heart and watch love appear in front of your eyes.
It's too many people expecting a good one, and not enough people being a good one.
A good one sees past your mistakes, makes you feel unstoppable,
And builds you up.
They challenge you and they keep you focused.
Devote quality time to the person you care for.
Genuinely invest in the things they are passionate about.
It doesn't have to be anything spectacular, all it has to be is thoughtful.

A woman who gives a man peace will never have to complain about not getting time.
A man who gives a woman consistency will never have to complain about loyalty.
It just takes more to be a good one.
If they don't invest in your passion, then they don't really believe in your potential.
If they don't contribute to your growth, then they are not meant to be in your future.
It's not about what they can do for you,
It's about what they can inspire you to do for yourself.
So maybe you're a good one, and maybe you're not.
But before you answer that ask yourself
If you could love someone like you.

WHOEVER YOU MAY BE

I'm tired of trying to figure out who is real and who is not.
I'm tired of spending every day wondering if love is really is what I believe it to be.
I'm tired of going through the motions and not taking chances.
I'm tired of allowing the pessimists to push me to the precipice.
It's frustrating feeling like I'm crazy for having hopes for something real.
I'm done with the runaround but never really getting anywhere.
I'm done with the people who just take and never give back.
I'm done with the fear and the resentment, and the baggage from the past.
I'm done with the fighting and arguing,
Because love isn't something we should have to bargain for.
It's disappointing feeling like I'm crazy for believing a relationship can last.
I'm through trying to make things work for the sake of having history.
I'm through trying to force myself to be content just because other people want to settle.
I'm through trying to turn potential into promise and never seeing results.
I'm through trying to prove I deserve to be trusted, when I wasn't the one who betrayed it.
It's disheartening feeling like every time I get something, I have to be scared of losing it.
I used to think that if you treated people a certain way then they would be genuine.
I used to think that giving somebody a fair chance would actually lead to real romance.

Hope For Love

I used to think that great love could happen whenever
I wanted it to.
I used to think that everybody had good intentions,
but I guess I thought wrong.
It's humbling realizing that everything isn't always as
simple as the movies make it seem.
I guess I'm learning that timing is everything. I'm
learning that happiness is a choice,
I'm learning that things happen when they're
supposed to,
And not always when we want them to.
I'm learning that just because I want it, that doesn't
mean it deserves me.
And it's crazy that after being tired and done, and
through,
I still believe in the possibilities of me and you,
Whoever you may be.

DREAM SOMEBODY

You ever had somebody special in your life?
Like they ain't have to tell you they were special,
You just knew.
It was something about them that you just couldn't put your finger on,
But that something had you thinking about them all the time.
That something had you hanging up the phone smiling for no reason.
Wishing you didn't have to leave for work and that you could cancel all your meetings.
Well maybe you don't...
At least not like I do,
Because I do all these things,
While I dream about you.

COMFORT ZONE

You can't be afraid to separate yourself.
You can't be afraid to chase your dreams and to go after what's in your heart.
I know it's not easy. I know it's hard when people misunderstand where you're trying to go.
But you can't give up.
You have to take a chance on you.
You don't get back the time that you wasted wishing you would've done things differently,
Or going back and reflecting on the mistakes that you made.
You have to accept where you are right now and make the best of it.
Change whatever you need to change.
Remove the people who you need to remove.
Do whatever you have to do to get ahead.

You cannot be afraid to separate yourself.
The more time you waste wishing life was different,
Or wishing you would've gone there, or would've talked to this person,
You're not doing anything but staying still.
And standing still only benefits a statue.

So, if you don't start moving, if you don't get active,
If you don't start building relationships and start talking to people,
You're never going to go anywhere.
You can't be afraid to separate yourself.
You don't need everybody to understand, it doesn't matter whether they get it.
It doesn't matter whether they respect it or not.
It doesn't matter if they acknowledge what you're doing.
All you have to do is put the work in for you.
If it feels right to you, keep going.
If you feel that's where you should be, stay there.
Don't change just because people don't get it.
You cannot be afraid to separate yourself.
You don't need everybody to get it to be great.
You don't need to be perfect to make a difference.
You don't need to be acknowledged to be important.
All you have to do is stay true to what's in your heart.
Don't be afraid to be different, don't be afraid to take a chance.
Greatness is right outside of your comfort zone.
Live better, dream bigger, and go further.
The only thing stopping you, is you.
You can't be afraid to separate yourself.

Whatever you're doing, and whatever you want to do,
Make sure you're giving it your all. I know the journey isn't easy.
Just don't quit.
Too many people pack up and walk away too soon.

Remember who you are. Don't let the process have you doubting yourself.
You are one prayer away from living your dream.
Embrace the ups, the twists, and the unexpected turns.
Don't run from the struggle, it's all there to strengthen and prepare you.
Growth is necessary.
Don't block your growth
Just because people don't understand where God is trying to take you.
You can't be afraid to separate yourself.
Choose greatness.

TEACH ME

I want to learn how to love you.
I am ready.
I am willing.
Teach me.

Rob Hill Sr.

I'VE BEEN THINKING ABOUT YOU

I hope something makes you laugh uncontrollably today.
I hope somebody makes you smile until your cheeks hurt.
I hope you feel incredibly beautiful, and capable of accomplishing anything.
I hope I'm the reason for your joy. And if not,
At least know that I've been thinking about you.

I hope you feel unstoppably happy and full of life.
I hope you begin to see what I see, and I hope you don't stop believing in your dreams.
I hope don't accept any excuses and I hope you make the best of every opportunity.
I hope that I'm the reason for your smile. But if not,
At least know that I've been thinking about you.

I hope you get that breakthrough you've been praying about.
I hope you're given a clean heart and that you hurt a little less than before.
I hope you experience something that gives you peace and more courage to believe.
And I hope that I'm the reason your heart is healed. But if not,
At least know that I've been thinking about you

Hope For Love

If by chance your smile begins to fade,
I hope you remember how much you deserve pure joy.
I hope your spirit dances with excitement for the future,
And I hope you know just how amazing you are.
So, if you somehow happen to see these words
I hope you know each one of them is directed at your heart.
And at least then you'll know,
I've been thinking about you.

HOPE FOR LOVE

A collection of poems for those who keep warmth in their heart when summer leaves.

ABOUT THE AUTHOR

Rob Hill Sr., affectionately known as the "Heart Healer," is an author, a proud Navy veteran, and entrepreneur originally from Chesapeake, Virginia. With a social following of nearly one million people, Rob is sought after internationally as a speaker on relationships, purpose-filled living, and community organizing. His writing has become a staple in the lives of those ready to live with purpose, passion, and principle. As he says, "We are all one choice away from a completely different life." His books—*About Something Real, For Single People, I Got You,* and *Truce: Healing Your Heart After Disappointment*—and further information about this "spirit on a mission" are available at RobHillSr.com.

Here's how you can connect with the author:

Website: robhillsr.com

Instagram: robhillsr

Twitter: @RobHillSr

Facebook: RobHillSr

SoundCloud: https://soundcloud.com/robhillsr

YouTube:

https://www.youtube.com/user/RobHillSr

Other Titles by Rob Hill, Sr.

FOR SINGLE PEOPLE WHO STILL UNDERSTAND THE VALUE OF RELATIONSHIPS

I GOT YOU

ABOUT SOMETHING REAL

TRUCE

THE MISSING PIECE

Made in the USA
Columbia, SC
01 February 2020

87335407R00093